Progress-Monitoring Assessments

Grade 2

![Houghton Mifflin Harcourt logo] HOUGHTON MIFFLIN HARCOURT

Contents

Purpose of the Progress-Monitoring Assessments   iv

Skills Tested in the Intervention Program   iv

Test Organization   vii

Administering the Assessments   ix

Scoring the Assessments   xi

Interpreting Test Results   xii

Test Results and Regrouping   xiii

Progress-Monitoring Chart   xiv

Progress-Monitoring Assessments

Lessons   1–2   1

Lessons   3–4   3

Lessons   5–6   5

Lessons   7–8   7

Lessons   9–10   9

Lessons   11–12   11

Lessons   13–14   13

Lessons   15–16   15

Lessons   17–18   18

Lessons   19–20   21

Lessons   21–22   25

Lessons   23–24   28

Lessons   25–26   32

Lessons   27–28   36

Lessons   29–30   40

Progress-Monitoring Assessments

The *Houghton Mifflin Harcourt Journeys* program provides intervention to support children who are having difficulty learning to read. The Progress-Monitoring Assessments provide biweekly checks on children's progress. The fifteen oral tests are administered individually and assess children's mastery of the high-frequency words and skills introduced in the prior two-week period.

Purpose of the Progress-Monitoring Assessments

- To check on a child's growth or problems in learning skills and high-frequency words
- To target learning gaps by using these test results combined with test results from the core instructional program

Skills Tested in the Intervention Program

Tested skills include
- Phonics
- High-Frequency Words
- Fluency and Comprehension

The charts on pages v and vi provide the list of tested phonics and high-frequency words. These skills are also taught in the core instructional program.

Contents of the Progress-Monitoring Assessments

Assessments for	Phonics and Structural Analysis Skills	High-Frequency Words (Words to Know)
Lessons 1–2	Short Vowels *a, i* CVC Words Short Vowels *o, u, e* Review CVC Words	around, until, five, take; do, children, use, comes
Lessons 3–4	Long Vowels *a, i* Hard and Soft Sounds for *c* Long Vowels *o, u, e* Hard and Soft Sounds for *g*	full, places, sing, city; today, see, cheer, mind
Lessons 5–6	Consonant Blends with *r, l, s* Common Final Blends *nd, ng, nk, nt, ft, xt, mp*	table, green, eat, cold; while, myself, work, second
Lessons 7–8	Double Consonants and *ck* Double Consonants (CVC) Consonant Digraphs *th, sh, wh, ch, tch, ph* Base Words with Endings *-s, -ed, -ing*	pictures, cried, told, air; eye, starts, high, open
Lessons 9–10	Base Words and Endings *-ed, -ing* CV Words Contractions	afraid, might, kept, many; better, because, own, really
Lessons 11–12	Base Words with Endings *-s, -es* Vowel Digraphs *ai, ay*	hard, another, far, heard; different, night, along, morning
Lessons 13–14	Vowel Digraphs *ee, ea* Long *o* (*o, oa, ow*)	story, world, everything, slowly; food, hair, started, warm
Lessons 15–16	Compound Words Schwa Vowel Sound Base Words and Endings *-ed, -ing*	after, thought, ever, off; something, river, saw, horse

v

Contents of the Progress-Monitoring Assessments (continued)

Assessments for	Phonics and Structural Analysis Skills	High-Frequency Words (Words to Know)
Lessons 17–18	Long *i* (*igh, ie, y*) Long *e* Sound for *y*	else, doing, teacher, studied; under, anything, words, soon
Lessons 19–20	*r*-Controlled Vowel *ar* *r*-Controlled Vowels *or, ore*	talk, sound, didn't, please; laugh, stood, begins, ready
Lessons 21–22	*r*-Controlled Vowel *er* *r*-Controlled Vowels *ir, ur* Homophones Base Words and Endings *-er, -est*	took, nothing, field, across; toward, floor, what's, found
Lessons 23–24	Suffixes *-y, -ly, -ful* Final Stable Syllables *-tion, -ture* Prefixes *re-, un-, over-, pre-, mis-* Silent Consonants	write, great, idea, without; earth, began, surprised, learning
Lessons 25–26	Words with /aw/: *au, aw, al, o, a* Vowel Diphthongs *oo, ew, ue, ou*	leaves, young, ball, learn; follow, don't, every, goes
Lessons 27–28	Vowel Diphthong *oo* Possessive nouns Vowel Diphthongs *ow, ou*	buy, tomorrow, outside, called; happened, enough, sorry, loved
Lessons 29–30	Reading Longer Words with long *a* and *i* Vowel Diphthongs *oi, oy* Reading Longer Words with long *o* and *e* Final Stable Syllable *-le*	woman, wash, once, who; years, door, remember, money

Test Organization

- There are fifteen biweekly assessments provided on blackline masters.
- For each assessment there is a teacher page followed by the child's test page with directions for ease of administering and scoring each test.
- Each assessment is divided into sections to test specific skills.
- This booklet also provides directions for administering and scoring each test. Guidelines for interpreting the results of the intervention program and reproducible record-keeping forms are included.

Sections on the Tests

A: Decodable Words This section measures a child's ability to read decodable words independently. The words target phonics and structural elements taught in the last two lessons. Words in each row target skills from a single week's lesson.

Directions: Read each of these words aloud.

fin	pat	lip	jam	sad
hog	set	bus	fun	web

B: High-Frequency Words Items in this section evaluate a child's ability to recognize high-frequency words taught in a two-week period. Each row assesses knowledge of words taught in a single week's lesson.

Directions: Read each of these words aloud.

around	until	five	take
do	children	use	comes

Lessons 1–14, C: Reading Sentences measures a child's ability to read sentences accurately. The sentences are a combination of decodable and familiar high-frequency words and become more complex as the year progresses.

Directions: Read each of these sentences aloud.

1. Jen got the kit to fix the cup.

2. She sat on top of the red rug.

3. Dad sat next to her to help with the kit.

4. Dad let Jen use the kit to fix the cup.

5. Jen gave Dad a big hug.

Lessons 15–30, C: Oral Reading of paragraphs measures a child's reading fluency, which is a combination of accuracy and rate. A comprehension question is included to evaluate the child's understanding of what is read. Fluency goals are based on below grade-level norms in order to measure progress with intervention instruction. Use grade-level fluency norms, along with observation and program assessment, to determine whether or not a child can transition out of intervention.

Administering the Assessments

Administer each assessment orally to individuals approximately every two weeks. The test should take three to five minutes.

Prepare one test form for children and a teacher's test form for each child being tested. Use it to record the child's responses and scores.

Materials Needed

- Child's test form
- Teacher's test form (one per child being tested)
- Stopwatch or watch or clock with a second hand (Oral Reading only)
- Clipboard (optional)

Keep in Mind

- Find a quiet place to give the test.

- Seat the child on the opposite side of a desk or table so that you can record responses inconspicuously.

- Tell the child that you want to learn how well he or she understands new sounds and words that the group has been learning. Explain that you will write down the child's responses to help you remember them.

- Give directions for each section, modifying them so that the child knows what to do.

- Give the child a reasonable time to respond.

- Stop testing if the child becomes frustrated or is unable to respond.

- Wait until the child has left to score or analyze responses.

To administer Decodable Words, High-Frequency Words (Sections A and B), **and Reading Sentences** (Section C, Lessons 1–14)**:**

- Ask the child to read each word or sentence aloud.

- Treat each word as a separate item.

- If a word is misread, write what the child said above the word.

- Draw a line through any words that are skipped, and insert words that the child adds. Mark self-corrections with an SC above the word.

To administer Oral Reading (Section C, Lessons 15–30)**:**

- Have a clock or watch with a second hand or a stopwatch available to time the child's reading.

- Explain that the test has two parts. First, you'll listen as the child reads the passage aloud. Then you'll ask a question about it. If the child does not know a word, remind him or her to use the letter-sounds.

- Time the child's reading for 30 seconds.

- If the child reads fewer than two of the first ten words, ask the child to stop. Write *discontinue* on the test form and a zero as the score.

- Draw a line through any mispronounced or omitted words. Write in words that the child inserts. Mark self-corrections with an SC above the word. (Self-corrections and repetitions will *not* be counted as errors.)

- Mark an X on the last word the child reads at the 30-second point.

- Allow the child to read to the end of the passage.

- Ask the comprehension question.

Scoring the Assessments

1. Obtain a child's raw score for each section by determining the number of words read correctly; record the score on the teacher's test form.

To determine accuracy scores:

- Treat each word as a separate item.

- Count mispronunciations, additions, and omissions as errors.

- Do not count repetitions or self-corrections as errors.

- Record the number of words read correctly.

To score fluency for oral reading passages:

- Determine errors made in reading for 30 seconds, using the guidelines for accuracy above.

- Determine words read correctly in 30 seconds by subtracting errors from the total words read.

- Multiply the words read correctly by 2 to determine the number of words read correctly per minute.

To score the comprehension questions:

- Evaluate the completeness of the child's answers.

- Give two points for a thorough answer. Give one point for an answer that was not detailed enough or that required prompting. Give no points if the child cannot or did not respond.

2. Use the child's scores to determine if the child is meeting the goals that are given for each section.

3. Use the test data and your observations to decide whether the child should move ahead or needs reteaching.

4. Record each child's scores across assessment periods on the Progress-Monitoring Chart. See the blackline masters on pages xiv–xv.

Interpreting Test Results

Use progress-monitoring test results plus core instruction assessments to make decisions about future intervention instruction. They will help you:

- determine if the child needs additional intervention or can be transitioned back to core instruction only

- evaluate the overall effectiveness of intervention by noting sufficient progress and learning

- adjust skill instruction to address specific learning gaps

Consider how a child's scores compare to the section goals. Decide if the child is benefiting from additional intervention.

☐ **Move Ahead** The child met goals for two or more sections.	☐ **Needs Reteaching** The child did not meet goals for two or more sections.

Adjusting Instruction

Analyze a child's errors and self-corrections in each section to identify problem areas and a starting point for reteaching, review, and extra practice.

- For phonics errors, provide additional word blending activities using word lists that feature target phonics skills. The goal here is for the child to be able to read approximately one word per second.

- For errors in recognizing high-frequency words, supply brief cumulative (approximately ten words) lists of high-frequency words to read and reread with increasing speed and accuracy.

- For improving rate, provide texts at a child's independent reading level for repeated or coached readings.

Test Results and Regrouping

Children in Strategic Intervention take part in the core instruction, activities, and assessments from *Houghton Mifflin Harcourt Journeys.* Test results from the Progress-Monitoring Assessments and Quick Check observations from the lessons indicate whether a child is benefiting from Strategic Intervention. Test results from other *Journeys* assessments provide data to help determine how to regroup children periodically.

Using *Houghton Mifflin Harcourt Journeys* Assessments	
Core Instructional Program Weekly and Unit Tests Benchmark and Fluency Tests	• Measure grade-level skill mastery and growth. • Use cut-off scores and professional judgment to regroup children who need intervention support.
Strategic Intervention Biweekly Progress-Monitoring Assessments	• Measures a child's gains as a result of Strategic Intervention instruction. • Use progress monitoring results as well as observations and program assessments to determine if child needs additional Strategic Intervention or should transition out of intervention or to more intensive intervention.

Progress-Monitoring Chart

Name _____ Teacher _____ School year _____

For each column, enter
+ (the child met the goal) or − (the child did not meet goal)

Progress Monitoring	Date Given	Decodable Words	High-Frequency Words	Reading Sentences	Actions		Comments
					Move Ahead	Needs Reteaching	
Lessons 1–2							
Lessons 3–4							
Lessons 5–6							
Lessons 7–8							
Lessons 9–10							
Lessons 11–12							
Lessons 13–14							

Progress-Monitoring Chart

Name _____

Teacher _____

School year _____

For each column, enter
+ (the child met the goal) or – (the child did not meet goal)

Progress Monitoring	Date Given	Decodable Words	High-Frequency Words	Oral Reading (Enter WCPM)	Comprehension	Actions			Comments
						Move Ahead	Needs Reteaching		
Lessons 15–16									
Lessons 17–18									
Lessons 19–20									
Lessons 21–22									
Lessons 23–24									
Lessons 25–26									
Lessons 27–28									
Lessons 29–30									

Decodable Words

Goal 8/10   Score _____ / 10

A.

fin	pat	lip	jam	sad
hog	set	bus	fun	web

High-Frequency Words

Goal 7/8   Score _____ / 8

B.

around	until	five	take
do	children	use	comes

Reading Sentences

Goal 37/42   Score _____ / 42

C.

1. Jen got the kit to fix the cup.

2. She sat on top of the red rug.

3. Dad sat next to her to help with the kit.

4. Dad let Jen use the kit to fix the cup.

5. Jen gave Dad a big hug.

☐ **Move Ahead** The child met goals for two or more sections.

☐ **Needs Reteaching** The child did not meet goals for two or more sections.

A.

fin	pat	lip	jam	sad
hog	set	bus	fun	web

B.

around	until	five	take
do	children	use	comes

C.

1. Jen got the kit to fix the cup.

2. She sat on top of the red rug.

3. Dad sat next to her to help with the kit.

4. Dad let Jen use the kit to fix the cup.

5. Jen gave Dad a big hug.

A. Decodable Words

Goal 8/10   Score _____ / 10

page	side	face	gate	Mike
tune	role	cube	here	poke

B. High-Frequency Words

Goal 7/8   Score _____ / 8

full	places	sing	city
today	see	cheer	mind

C. Reading Sentences

Goal 32/37   Score _____ / 37

1. How do you get to school?

2. Do you take a bus or ride a bike?

3. Do you sit with Mom in a van?

4. Do you walk with other children?

5. Name five ways you can get to school.

☐ **Move Ahead** The child met goals for two or more sections.

☐ **Needs Reteaching** The child did not meet goals for two or more sections.

A.

page	side	face	gate	Mike
tune	role	cube	here	poke

B.

full	places	sing	city
today	see	cheer	mind

C.

1. How do you get to school?

2. Do you take a bus or ride a bike?

3. Do you sit with Mom in a van?

4. Do you walk with other children?

5. Name five ways you can get to school.

Decodable Words

Goal 8/10   Score _____ / 10

A.

drop	glide	left	flame	crane
ramp	ring	gift	band	dunk

High-Frequency Words

Goal 7/8   Score _____ / 8

B.

table	green	eat	cold
while	myself	work	second

Reading Sentences

Goal 35/40   Score _____ / 40

C.

1. Ant dug a little hole in the sand.

2. He did not dig fast, but he was glad.

3. Bear dug a big hole next to a tree.

4. He was cold, but he did not stop.

5. Both animals had made a home.

☐ **Move Ahead** The child met goals for two or more sections.

☐ **Needs Reteaching** The child did not meet goals for two or more sections.

A.

drop	glide	left	flame	crane
ramp	ring	gift	band	dunk

B.

table	green	eat	cold
while	myself	work	second

C.

1. Ant dug a little hole in the sand.

2. He did not dig fast, but he was glad.

3. Bear dug a big hole next to a tree.

4. He was cold, but he did not stop.

5. Both animals had made a home.

Decodable Words

Goal 8/10   Score _____ / 10

A.

back	fell	chill	luck	thick
itch	white	takes	washing	locked

High-Frequency Words

Goal 7/8   Score _____ / 8

B.

pictures	cried	told	air
eye	starts	high	open

Reading Sentences

Goal 42/47   Score _____ / 47

C.

1. There is a lot we can do at home.

2. We can sit in the pretty green grass.

3. We can play tag and catch.

4. We can use the phone to say hello.

5. We can bake a cake for Mom and Dad.

6. It is fun to be at home!

☐ **Move Ahead** The child met goals for two or more sections.   ☐ **Needs Reteaching** The child did not meet goals for two or more sections.

A.

back	fell	chill	luck	thick
itch	white	takes	washing	locked

B.

pictures	cried	told	air
eye	starts	high	open

C.

1. There is a lot we can do at home.

2. We can sit in the pretty green grass.

3. We can play tag and catch.

4. We can use the phone to say hello.

5. We can bake a cake for Mom and Dad.

6. It is fun to be at home!

Name _____   Date _____

A. Decodable Words

Goal 8/10   Score _____ / 10

taking	named	chased	shaping	fixed
can't	I'm	won't	we'd	I'd

B. High-Frequency Words

Goal 7/8   Score _____ / 8

afraid	might	kept	many
better	because	own	really

C. Reading Sentences

Goal 42/47   Score _____ / 47

1. "Would you take a picture of this fish?"
Ben asked Mom.

2. "Don't you want to be in the picture?"
asked Mom.

3. Ben went up to the glass to see the fish.

4. It showed its big, white teeth as it went by.

5. Ben smiled and said, "I'll pass!"

☐ **Move Ahead** The child met goals for two or more sections.	☐ **Needs Reteaching** The child did not meet goals for two or more sections.

A.

taking	named	chased	shaping	fixed
can't	I'm	won't	we'd	I'd

B.

afraid	might	kept	many
better	because	own	really

C.

1. "Would you take a picture of this fish?"
   Ben asked Mom.

2. "Don't you want to be in the picture?"
   asked Mom.

3. Ben went up to the glass to see the fish.

4. It showed its big, white teeth as it went by.

5. Ben smiled and said, "I'll pass!"

Decodable Words

Goal 8/10   Score _____ / 10

A.

naps	foxes	kites	wishes	jobs
day	wait	stay	fail	clay

High-Frequency Words

Goal 7/8   Score _____ / 8

B.

hard	another	far	heard
different	night	along	morning

Reading Sentences

Goal 39/44   Score _____ / 44

C.

1. There are a lot of fun games that children play.

2. You can chase someone in a game of tag.

3. You can play games with a jump rope.

4. You can hide and hope someone can't find you.

5. Can you think of some more fun games?

☐ **Move Ahead** The child met goals for two or more sections.

☐ **Needs Reteaching** The child did not meet goals for two or more sections.

A.

naps	foxes	kites	wishes	jobs
day	wait	stay	fail	clay

B.

hard	another	far	heard
different	night	along	morning

C.

1. There are a lot of fun games that children play.

2. You can chase someone in a game of tag.

3. You can play games with a jump rope.

4. You can hide and hope someone can't find you.

5. Can you think of some more fun games?

Decodable Words

Goal 8/10   Score _____ / 10

A.

meat	tree	beam	leap	greet
goal	coat	show	loan	blow

High-Frequency Words

Goal 7/8   Score _____ / 8

B.

story	world	everything	slowly
food	hair	started	warm

Reading Sentences

Goal 47/52   Score _____ / 52

C.

1. Pat handed me a note in class.

2. She asked if I would go to her party.

3. Pat lived on a big boat that was her home.

4. I could not wait to see her boat.

5. I did not think Pat would ask me to go.

6. It was nice to know she liked me!

☐ **Move Ahead** The child met goals for two or more sections. | ☐ **Needs Reteaching** The child did not meet goals for two or more sections.

A.

meat	tree	beam	leap	greet
goal	coat	show	loan	blow

B.

story	world	everything	slowly
food	hair	started	warm

C.

1. Pat handed me a note in class.

2. She asked if I would go to her party.

3. Pat lived on a big boat that was her home.

4. I could not wait to see her boat.

5. I did not think Pat would ask me to go.

6. It was nice to know she liked me!

Decodable Words

Goal 8/10 Score _____ / 10

A.

rainbow	baseball	alike	driveway	ahead
nodded	robbing	tagged	sipping	flapped

High-Frequency Words

Goal 7/8 Score _____ / 8

B.

after	thought	ever	off
something	river	saw	horse

GO ON ➡

Name _____ Date _____

Oral Reading Have the child read the title and the entire passage. Start timing when the child begins reading. Make an X in the text at 30 seconds.

C.

The Zoo	2
It is fun to go to the zoo. You can see	13
the animals. There are big cats at the zoo.	22
They sit in the sun. They like to sleep all	32
day. There are bears. They are big and	40
black. They play outside.	44
Some zoos have trains. You can sit in	52
the train. The train goes around the zoo.	60
You can look at the animals. You do not	69
have to walk.	72
There are big zoos. There are small	79
zoos. Some zoos have a lot of animals.	87
Some do not. Zoos are all a lot of fun!	97

Comprehension Questions

1. *Why is it fun to go to the zoo?* (You can look at all the animals.)
2. *Why do some zoos have trains?* (You can see the animals without walking.)

Fluency Score	**Comprehension Score**	**How to Score Questions**
Total words correctly read in 30 seconds _____ X 2	Score _____ /2	2 = full credit answer 1 = partial credit answer 0 = incorrect/unanswered
Goal 13–33 WCPM Score _____	Goal = 1/2	

☐ **Move Ahead** The child met goals for two or more sections.

☐ **Needs Reteaching** The child did not meet goals for two or more sections.

A.

rainbow	baseball	alike	driveway	ahead
nodded	robbing	tagged	sipping	flapped

B.

after	thought	ever	off
something	river	saw	horse

C.

The Zoo

It is fun to go to the zoo. You can see the animals. There are big cats at the zoo. They sit in the sun. They like to sleep all day. There are bears. They are big and black. They play outside.

Some zoos have trains. You can sit in the train. The train goes around the zoo. You can look at the animals. You do not have to walk.

There are big zoos. There are small zoos. Some zoos have a lot of animals. Some do not. Zoos are all a lot of fun!

Name _____ Date _____

A. Decodable Words

Goal 8/10   Score _____ / 10

right	tie	try	by	sigh
baby	cities	carry	hurries	furry

B. High-Frequency Words

Goal 7/8   Score _____ / 8

else	doing	teacher	studied
under	anything	words	soon

GO ON ➡

Oral Reading Have the child read the title and the entire passage. Start timing when the child begins reading. Make an X in the text at 30 seconds.

C.

A Bad Day	3
Tom had a bad day. He got up late this	13
morning. He could not find his shoe. Tom	21
did not have time to eat. He ran for the	31
bus, but he missed it. Then he had to walk	41
to school.	43
Tom's day did not get any better. He	51
left his lunch at home. He also lost his	60
book. Tom was very sad. What a bad day!	69
Tom walked home after school. He told	76
his mother about his day. His mother sat	84
with him. She gave him something to eat.	92
She told him a joke to make him smile. Tom	102
felt better.	104

Comprehension Questions

1. *Why does Tom have a bad day?* (Everything goes wrong for Tom.)
2. *How does Tom's mother help him feel better?* (She spends time with him and makes him smile.)

Fluency Score	**Comprehension Score**	**How to Score Questions**
Total words correctly read in 30 seconds _____ X 2	Score _____ /2	2 = full credit answer
		1 = partial credit answer
Goal 13–33 WCPM Score _____	Goal = 1/2	0 = incorrect/unanswered

☐ **Move Ahead** The child met goals for two or more sections.	☐ **Needs Reteaching** The child did not meet goals for two or more sections.

A.

right	tie	try	by	sigh
baby	cities	carry	hurries	furry

B.

else	doing	teacher	studied
under	anything	words	soon

C.

A Bad Day

Tom had a bad day. He got up late this morning. He could not find his shoe. Tom did not have time to eat. He ran for the bus, but he missed it. Then he had to walk to school.

Tom's day did not get any better. He left his lunch at home. He also lost his book. Tom was very sad. What a bad day!

Tom walked home after school. He told his mother about his day. His mother sat with him. She gave him something to eat. She told him a joke to make him smile. Tom felt better.

Decodable Words

A.

star	yard	carve	barn	farm
score	torch	storm	fork	chore

High-Frequency Words

B.

talk	sound	didn't	please
laugh	stood	begins	ready

GO ON

Oral Reading Have the child read the title and the entire passage. Start timing when the child begins reading. Make an X in the text at 30 seconds.

C.

All in a Day's Work	5
Most people think of dogs as pets. But	13
dogs can work. They can do things that	21
help people.	23
Did you know that dogs can save lives?	31
They can smell very well. They can find	39
people who are lost. These people may be	47
hurt or sick. Dogs can find them so they	56
can get help.	59
Dogs can also help find bad people.	66
These people hide. They do not want to	74
get caught. Dogs can smell them. They	81
can show where these people hide.	87
Dogs can help people who are sick.	94
People smile when they pet dogs. They	101
have fun when they play with dogs. This	109
helps people feel better.	113
Dogs do good work. They help people	120
a lot.	122

Comprehension Questions

1. *How can dogs help people?* (They can find people and help sick people feel better.)
2. *How are dogs able to find people?* (They can smell very well.)

Fluency Score	**Comprehension Score**	**How to Score Questions**
Total words correctly read in 30 seconds _____ X 2	Score _____ /2	2 = full credit answer
		1 = partial credit answer
Goal 13–33 WCPM Score _____	Goal = 1/2	0 = incorrect/unanswered

☐ **Move Ahead** The child met goals for two or more sections.	☐ **Needs Reteaching** The child did not meet goals for two or more sections.

A.

star	yard	carve	barn	farm
score	torch	storm	fork	chore

B.

talk	sound	didn't	please
laugh	stood	begins	ready

GO ON

C.

All in a Day's Work

Most people think of dogs as pets. But dogs can work. They can do things that help people.

Did you know that dogs can save lives? They can smell very well. They can find people who are lost. These people may be hurt or sick. Dogs can find them so they can get help.

Dogs can also help find bad people. These people hide. They do not want to get caught. Dogs can smell them. They can show where these people hide.

Dogs can help people who are sick. People smile when they pet dogs. They have fun when they play with dogs. This helps people feel better.

Dogs do good work. They help people a lot.

Decodable Words

Goal 8/10   Score _____ / 10

A.

tiger	butter	girl	bird	curves
hardest	banned	band	hottest	fatter

High-Frequency Words

Goal 7/8   Score _____ / 8

B.

took	nothing	field	across
toward	floor	what's	found

GO ON ➤

Oral Reading Have the child read the title and the entire passage. Start timing when the child begins reading. Make an X in the text at 30 seconds.

C.

A New Friend	3
Kim was new at school last year.	10
She sat by herself and did not talk. The	19
teacher asked us to be nice to Kim. We did	29
not know her. What would we say to her?	38
We all ate lunch. Kim sat by herself	46
again. Then we went out to play. Kim sat	55
on a swing. She did not want to play. Kim	65
missed her old home. She looked sad.	72
I sat on a swing next to Kim and told	82
her my name. We watched the game and	90
talked. Kim was nice. We had a lot of fun.	100
Kim and I are friends now. We play all	109
the time. I am glad she moved here!	117

Comprehension Questions

1. *Why does the teacher ask the class to be nice to Kim?* (Kim is new and she does not have any friends.)

2. *Why is Kim sad?* (Kim feels sad because she misses her old home.)

Fluency Score	**Comprehension Score**	**How to Score Questions**
Total words correctly read in 30 seconds _____ X 2	Score _____ /2	2 = full credit answer
		1 = partial credit answer
Goal 13–33 WCPM Score _____	Goal = 1/2	0 = incorrect/unanswered

☐ **Move Ahead** The child met goals for two or more sections.	☐ **Needs Reteaching** The child did not meet goals for two or more sections.

A.

tiger	butter	girl	bird	curves
hardest	banned	band	hottest	fatter

B.

took	nothing	field	across
toward	floor	what's	found

C.

A New Friend

Kim was new at school last year. She sat by herself and did not talk. The teacher asked us to be nice to Kim. We did not know her. What would we say to her?

We all ate lunch. Kim sat by herself again. Then we went out to play. Kim sat on a swing. She did not want to play. Kim missed her old home. She looked sad.

I sat on a swing next to Kim and told her my name. We watched the game and talked. Kim was nice. We had a lot of fun.

Kim and I are friends now. We play all the time. I am glad she moved here!

Decodable Words

A.

Goal 8/10   Score _____ / 10

only	future	station	grassy	hopeful
unlock	overtime	preset	remake	mistake

High-Frequency Words

B.

Goal 7/8   Score _____ / 8

write	great	idea	without
earth	began	surprised	learning

GO ON ➡

Oral Reading Have the child read the title and the entire passage. Start timing when the child begins reading. Make an X in the text at 30 seconds.

C.

A Piece of Cake	4
Do you know how to make a cake?	12
It takes a long time. There is a lot to do.	23
First, you put in eggs and butter. You add	32
other things, too. Then you bake it. It can	41
take a long time to cook. The cake smells	50
good!	51
After it bakes, the cake is hot. You	59
must let it get cool. It can be hard to wait.	70
It looks so good. When it is cool, you put	80
the icing on it. This is the fun part. You can	91
make the cake look pretty. Now the cake is	100
ready to eat.	103
Have a friend come over. Give your	110
friend a piece of cake. Cake tastes better	118
with a friend!	121

Comprehension Questions

1. *How do you make a cake?* (You add things together and bake it.)
2. *Why does the cake need to cool?* (It is too hot to put icing on it.)

Fluency Score	**Comprehension Score**	**How to Score Questions**
Total words correctly read in 30 seconds ___ X 2 Goal 13–33 WCPM Score _____	Score ___ /2 Goal = 1/2	2 = full credit answer 1 = partial credit answer 0 = incorrect/unanswered
☐ **Move Ahead** The child met goals for two or more sections.		☐ **Needs Reteaching** The child did not meet goals for two or more sections.

A.

| only | future | station | grassy | hopeful |
| unlock | overtime | preset | remake | mistake |

B.

| write | great | idea | without |
| earth | began | surprised | learning |

GO ON

C.

A Piece of Cake

Do you know how to make a cake? It takes a long time. There is a lot to do. First, you put in eggs and butter. You add other things, too. Then you bake it. It can take a long time to cook. The cake smells good!

After it bakes, the cake is hot. You must let it get cool. It can be hard to wait. It looks so good. When it is cool, you put the icing on it. This is the fun part. You can make the cake look pretty. Now the cake is ready to eat.

Have a friend come over. Give your friend a piece of cake. Cake tastes better with a friend!

A. Decodable Words

Goal 8/10   Score _____ / 10

chalk	hawk	fault	draw	haul
stew	group	glue	blew	boot

B. High-Frequency Words

Goal 7/8   Score _____ / 8

leaves	young	ball	learn
follow	don't	every	goes

GO ON

Oral Reading Have the child read the title and the entire passage. Start timing when the child begins reading. Make an X in the text at 30 seconds.

C.

A Little Plant	3
Jim came home from school. He had a	11
little plant.	13
"What is that?" asked Jim's mother.	19
"It is my little plant," said Jim. "I got it	29
at school today. I will put it in the ground.	39
Then I will watch it grow."	45
"That sounds like fun," said Jim's	51
mother. "Tell me if you need help."	58
Jim went to the yard. He made a little	67
hole. He put his little plant in the hole.	76
Then Jim put some water in the hole.	84
Now Jim knew that the plant could	91
grow. But it would take time for it to get	101
big. Jim would watch the plant every day.	109
He would watch it for weeks.	115
Jim went inside. "My plant will be the	123
best one ever!" he told his mother.	130

Comprehension Questions

1. *What does Jim do in the story?* (He gets a plant and puts it in the ground.)
2. *Why does Jim put water in the hole?* (The plant needs water to grow.)

Fluency Score	**Comprehension Score**	**How to Score Questions**
Total words correctly read in 30 seconds _____ X 2	Score _____ /2	2 = full credit answer
		1 = partial credit answer
Goal 43–63 WCPM Score _____	Goal = 1/2	0 = incorrect/unanswered

☐ **Move Ahead** The child met goals for two or more sections.	☐ **Needs Reteaching** The child did not meet goals for two or more sections.

A.

chalk	hawk	fault	draw	haul
stew	group	glue	blew	boot

B.

leaves	young	ball	learn
follow	don't	every	goes

GO ON

C.

A Little Plant

Jim came home from school. He had a little plant.

"What is that?" asked Jim's mother.

"It is my little plant," said Jim. "I got it at school today. I will put it in the ground. Then I will watch it grow."

"That sounds like fun," said Jim's mother. "Tell me if you need help."

Jim went to the yard. He made a little hole. He put his little plant in the hole. Then Jim put some water in the hole.

Now Jim knew that the plant could grow. But it would take time for it to get big. Jim would watch the plant every day. He would watch it for weeks.

Jim went inside. "My plant will be the best one ever!" he told his mother.

Decodable Words

Goal 8/10   Score _____ / 10

A.

cook	shook	man's	look	books'
brown	touch	shout	crowd	loud

High-Frequency Words

Goal 7/8   Score _____ / 8

B.

buy	tomorrow	outside	called
happened	enough	sorry	loved

GO ON ➤

Name _____ Date _____

Oral Reading Have the child read the title and the entire passage. Start timing when the child begins reading. Make an X in the text at 30 seconds.

C.

A Big World	3
The world is a big place. There is a lot	13
to see. It is fun to learn about our world.	23
We can learn about the fish in the sea.	32
There are many fish in the water. They swim	41
under our boats. Some fish are big. Some	49
are little. Some look funny. Some look mean.	57
What fish do you want to learn about?	65
We can learn about the stars in the sky.	74
We see them when it is dark. They look like	84
little lights in the night. Why are they there?	93
We can learn about how other people	100
live. We do not all look the same. We do	110
not all do things the same way. It is fun to	121
see how people can be different.	127
What do you want to learn about first?	135

Comprehension Questions

1. *In the story, what things can you learn about?* (You can learn about fish, stars, and people.)

2. *What is one thing you learned in this story?* (There are many different fish. Stars shine in the dark. People are all different.)

Fluency Score	**Comprehension Score**	**How to Score Questions**
Total words correctly read in 30 seconds _____ X 2	Score _____ /2	2 = full credit answer
		1 = partial credit answer
Goal 43–63 WCPM Score _____	Goal = 1/2	0 = incorrect/unanswered

☐ **Move Ahead** The child met goals for two or more sections.	☐ **Needs Reteaching** The child did not meet goals for two or more sections.

A.

cook	shook	man's	look	books'
brown	touch	shout	crowd	loud

B.

buy	tomorrow	outside	called
happened	enough	sorry	loved

GO ON ➤

C.

A Big World

The world is a big place. There is a lot to see. It is fun to learn about our world.

We can learn about the fish in the sea. There are many fish in the water. They swim under our boats. Some fish are big. Some are little. Some look funny. Some look mean. What fish do you want to learn about?

We can learn about the stars in the sky. We see them when it is dark. They look like little lights in the night. Why are they there?

We can learn about how other people live. We do not all look the same. We do not all do things the same way. It is fun to see how people can be different.

What do you want to learn about first?

A. Decodable Words

Goal 8/10   Score _____ / 10

played	coil	light	painter	enjoy
fable	turtle	candle	shown	oatmeal

B. High-Frequency Words

Goal 7/8   Score _____ / 8

woman	wash	once	who
years	door	remember	money

GO ON

Oral Reading Have the child read the title and the entire passage. Start timing when the child begins reading. Make an X in the text at 30 seconds.

C.

A Camping Trip	3
Last week was a lot of fun. My family	12
and I went camping. We went for a walk in	22
the woods. It was a nice day. The sun was	32
shining. We saw lots of animals. They ran	40
fast! I pointed to a big red tree. It looked	50
different from the others. My father told	57
me it was a red maple tree.	64
Then we stopped to have lunch. After	71
lunch, my father said he lost the map. Oh,	80
no! We were lost. We tried to walk back	89
the way we came. It did not work. My	98
father said we were walking in circles. My	106
sister started to cry.	110
Then I saw the big red tree! I pointed	119
to it and told my father. He knew how to	129
get back from there. We were so glad to	138
see the camp!	141

Comprehension Questions

1. *What is the problem in the story?* (The family gets lost in the woods.)
2. *How does the family find its way back?* (They find the big red tree again.)

Fluency Score	**Comprehension Score**	**How to Score Questions**
Total words correctly read in 30 seconds _____ X 2	Score _____ /2	2 = full credit answer
		1 = partial credit answer
Goal 43–63 WCPM Score _____	Goal = 1/2	0 = incorrect/unanswered
☐ **Move Ahead** The child met goals for two or more sections.	☐ **Needs Reteaching** The child did not meet goals for two or more sections.	

A.

| played | coil | light | painter | enjoy |
| fable | turtle | candle | shown | oatmeal |

B.

| woman | wash | once | who |
| years | door | remember | money |

GO ON ➡

C.

A Camping Trip

Last week was a lot of fun. My family and I went camping. We went for a walk in the woods. It was a nice day. The sun was shining. We saw lots of animals. They ran fast! I pointed to a big red tree. It looked different from the others. My father told me it was a red maple tree.

Then we stopped to have lunch. After lunch, my father said he lost the map. Oh, no! We were lost. We tried to walk back the way we came. It did not work. My father said we were walking in circles. My sister started to cry.

Then I saw the big red tree! I pointed to it and told my father. He knew how to get back from there. We were so glad to see the camp!